WELCOME TO DOUNE CASTLE

Doune Castle was built in the late 1300s by Robert Stewart, 1st Duke of Albany, Earl of Menteith and Fife. Younger brother of the ineffectual Robert III, he was ruler of Scotland in all but name from 1388 until his death in 1420. He is known to history as the 'uncrowned king', and his seat at Doune was virtually a royal castle.

Situated on a wooded bend, where the Ardoch Burn flows into the River Teith, the castle's position is naturally strong, and its design is a testament to the Duke of Albany's power. However, where it was once thought that the castle originated entirely from Albany's vision, new research suggests that he may have been working with existing structures. Over the last few years, surveys and excavations have been undertaken around the site, and we are constantly gaining new information about its history and use. Some information in this guide is therefore at odds with previous thinking.

Above: One of the many mason's marks left by craftsmen on the walls of the castle.

Opposite: Spiral staircases lead to rooms and viewpoints at the top of Doune's towers.

CONTENTS

HIGHLIGHTS

THE CASTLE WALLS AND BEYOND

◀ GARGOYLES
The waterspouts lining the courtyard wall of the great hall have been carved with characterful faces. They date from the restoration in the 1880s (p.11).

▲ THE GATEHOUSE TOWER
The imposing structure of the gatehouse tower dominates the castle's exterior. It also houses what would have been the castle's most sumptuous apartments (p.6).

▼ A WALK BY THE TEITH
A major source of salmon fishing for centuries, the Teith now provides a picturesque and peaceful backdrop to the castle (p.30).

INSIDE THE CASTLE

▶ MEDIEVAL GRANDEUR
Doune perfectly demonstrates how a medieval nobleman built his residence to impress his contemporaries (p.20).

▶ NOOKS AND CRANNIES
The castle is full of hidden corners and small chambers to be explored by visitors. Their possible functions have been much debated by historians and archaeologists (p.22).

◄ THE BONNY EARL
Keeper of Doune Castle in the 1590s, James Stewart, 2nd Lord Doune and 2nd Earl of Moray, was murdered by the Marquis of Huntly. The event, and the castle, have been remembered in the folk ballad 'The Bonny Earl of Murray' (p.43).

▼ A DARING ESCAPE
After the Battle of Falkirk in 1746, the Jacobites gathered and held their prisoners at Doune. Several made a plucky escape from within these walls (p.44).

▲ MONTY PYTHON
The comedy troupe Monty Python's Flying Circus came to Doune to film their famous adventure *Monty Python and the Holy Grail*, and the castle has attracted film fans ever since (p.46).

◄ A VIEW FROM THE TOP OF THE TOWER
From here you can see why Doune's position was so strong – it was surrounded by water, and from its highest point you could see, and be seen, for miles around (p.25).

◄ VICTORIAN RESTORATION
Extensively restored in the 1880s, the castle is a physical demonstration of the Victorian fascination with the medieval past (p.23).

DOUNE CASTLE AT A GLANCE

Dominated by its imposing towers and high curtain walls, Doune Castle feels like a space of peace and safety. However, its courtyard would once have been bustling with servants and nobles conducting their day-to-day lives. Much of the castle retains its medieval layout, and its rooms were formed for medieval functions.

Ground floor   1st floor   2nd floor

1 ENTRANCE PASSAGE

The main means of entering the castle, with a guardroom leading off it.

2 CELLARS

Ground-floor rooms used for storing food and drink. This would include provisions and rent collected in kind from the surrounding area.

3 POSSIBLE PIT PRISON

Often thought to be another storage cellar, this may well have been a prison, into which people would be lowered from a chamber adjoining the duke's hall.

4 SITE OF POSSIBLE SOUTH RANGE

It used to be thought that this range was never completed, but experts now believe that there were once buildings along this wall, with a chapel at the south-east corner.

5 SERVERY

A room through which food would be passed from the kitchen to servants working in the great hall.

6 KITCHEN

The main area in which food would have been prepared, dominated by its large fireplace.

7 GREAT HALL

The main eating area within the castle, for servants and guests. Some minor servants would also have slept here.

8 DUKE'S HALL

A more private space in which the duke could receive guests, dine and conduct his affairs. Extensively restored in the 1880s.

9 DUKE'S STUDY

Formerly thought to be the duke's bedchamber. We now think this was probably the duke's private study.

10 'MARY QUEEN OF SCOTS' BEDCHAMBER'

A fine bedchamber, suitable for important guests, but probably used by the steward or chamberlain of the castle most of the time.

11 CLOSETS

Two small chambers leading off the bedchamber. One was a latrine closet, while we are unsure of the purpose of the other. Used as cells in the castle's later period.

12 UPPER HALL

Probably the duke's main bedchamber, as well as a place in which he could have conducted business.

13 ORATORY

A small, private chapel for the duke and his intimate family and guests.

14 CHAMBER

Possibly an antechamber for those waiting to see the duke in the upper hall.

15 WALL WALK

Battlements at the top of the curtain walls, allowing guards a clear view of the surrounding land.

This page: The gatehouse tower, with its fine windows and circular drum tower, was built both for comfort and defence, and would have been a powerful symbol of Albany's status.

THE GATEHOUSE TOWER

The imposing gatehouse tower houses the principal apartments of the duke and duchess, as well as the main access to the castle. It is an imposing structure and visually represents the power of the castle's owner.

Above the entranceway you can see several large windows. These provided light to the high-status chambers within the tower. More chambers are contained within the circular, or drum, tower to your left.

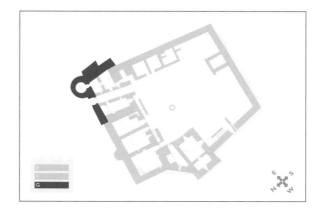

From outside the entrance, you can see the first hints that Albany was not solely responsible for the castle's construction. The arch appears to have been rebuilt, indicating that it was built at a different time from the uprights. Looking straight along the passageway, you will notice that it does not follow a straight course but instead curves to the right. This suggests that Albany was working around pre-existing structures when constructing his residence.

All entrances were potential weak spots and so the main doorway was provided with significant defences. Something similar to the wooden door you see today probably existed in the past, and the iron yett, or gate, just behind the door is the medieval original. Such yetts were common features of Scottish castles, acting as an extra line of protection should the door be breached.

You can also see the remainder of a timber drawbar, which would have secured the door. The date of this timber is not known, but such a massive defence would have been difficult to install after the gatehouse was completed, so it was probably part of the initial building work. Immediately above you at the door is a long narrow slit in the roof. This was a murder hole, and allowed defenders to drop projectiles on intruders. You will see the access to this hole in the duke's hall later in the tour.

THE ENTRANCE PASSAGE AND CHAMBERS

This passage provided the main access to the castle and was the principal way of controlling who entered and when. The layers of defence in place show that Albany wanted the castle to appear strong and easily defensible.

If the first doorway and yett were breached, an attacker would have still more obstacles to overcome. Originally the passage had a second door about halfway along and yet another yett at the far end. The presence of several barriers was also symbolic, emphasising that visitors were entering the private space of a powerful individual. The defences would have added to the theatricality of the entranceway, heightening the contrast between the long, gloomy passage and the open courtyard. Given how infrequently Doune was called upon to defend itself, this symbolism was probably at least as important as the actual defensive function.

Leading off the passage are several small chambers. The chamber now serving as the castle shop was probably a guardroom or porter's lodge. The fish-tailed arrow-slit (another early feature suggesting that the construction of the castle may have begun in the 1200s) would have provided a way to defend the passage. The small room off the shop, now a storeroom, may have been a prison cell, allowing the porter or guard to watch over anyone the duke was holding.

Left: The entrance passage, which provided the main access to the castle and was the principal way of controlling who entered and when. The way it curves slightly has been seen as evidence that Albany was incorporating pre-existing structures into his castle.

The entrances to the shop and to this store also provide clues to extensive remodelling in the castle's past. The doors have been altered, indicating that at some point the purpose of these rooms changed. Indeed, the stonework on the storeroom doorway is good quality, suggesting that it was not intended to be a door between a prison cell and guardroom.

On the opposite side of the entrance passage lie three chambers which, for security, were originally accessed from the courtyard. They probably provided storage, with the hatch in the first room allowing food or drink to be sent directly to the duke's hall. Recent analysis suggests that the wall between the first two chambers is a later addition, and that there were originally only two chambers, with a door connecting them. This may explain why there is no hatch in the middle chamber.

The small circular room which forms the lowest level of the tower was once thought to be a well, but this was disproved by archaeological investigation in the 1980s. The hatch access makes it possible it was used to store food. However, the current doorway has been altered, and either did not originally exist or was considerably smaller than it is now. This suggests it may once have been a pit prison, for gaoling low-status wrongdoers.

Above: The yett, or gate, is the medieval original.

THE COURTYARD AND CELLARS

This page: Doune's central courtyard is now its defining feature. However, it would once have felt very different, with buildings filling much of the space we see today.

The contrast between the enclosed passageway and the open space of the courtyard is a startling one, but the medieval visitor would have had a very different experience from the one we have today.

The courtyard would most likely have had a dirt or cobbled floor (cobbles have been found under the grass, but have not been dated) and would have been much more cramped than it is now. It was long thought that Albany never finished building the castle and that there were no buildings along the south range of the courtyard. However, recent work has suggested the opposite.

To your left as you enter the courtyard you will see the remains of stone buildings along the courtyard's east range. We cannot be sure of their date and function, but it is possible that at least part of them pre-date the existing curtain wall. On the south range, we can see windows, suggesting that there may once have been fine accommodation here (see illustration page 12).

The courtyard would have been much more crowded than it is now. The buildings along the north and west ranges are all that survive to show what it would have been like. Many of the lost buildings would have been used by servants, making the courtyard a hive of activity.

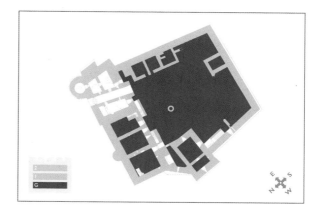

Off the courtyard on the north range there are three cellars for storing the vast quantity of food and drink needed to supply a household the size of the Duke of Albany's. They also stored the rents from the estate in which were normally paid in the form of meat and grain. The cellars at either end contain access to the floor above, allowing food and drink to be delivered straight to the great hall.

The stair in the eastern store emerges at the dais end of the hall, a raised area where the duke sat during meals, so this may have been the wine cellar. At the other end, the access emerges at the service end of the hall, suggesting that it transported lower-status goods, perhaps ale, with the middle room acting as the bread store. The kitchen tower also had storage space on the ground floor. These rooms are now used by Historic Scotland's Monument Conservation Unit.

The gargoyles around the inner walls of the courtyard date from the 1880s. These decorative water spouts depict a variety of animals, and are designed to drain water away from the side of the building. They seem to have replaced simpler spouts in the same positions.

Left: Animal gargoyles in the courtyard. They were added during the 1880s, and were designed to drain water away from the castle's walls.

THE CURTAIN WALLS

This page: The castle as it might have looked in Albany's day, with buildings along all four ranges of the courtyard. Evidence suggests that at least some of these buildings were completed, contrary to what was previously thought.

The curtain walls which now define the courtyard space suggest many complexities in the development of the castle, and give clues to hidden aspects of its history.

The massive walls are impressive, but defence was not their only function. The fine windows in the south range, opposite you as you enter the courtyard, were probably designed to provide maximum light to grand chambers built against this wall. A close examination of the windows supports this idea. There is evidence that they were glazed and furnished with iron grilles. There would be no reason to put such expensive finishing touches on incomplete rooms. The lack of evidence on the surviving wall may be due to restoration in the 1880s.

We know from records that Albany used Doune on several occasions to host large gatherings of high-ranking guests. If the only accommodation available was what we see today, there would simply not have been enough room to house everyone according to their status. This suggests that some of the buildings on the south range must have been used to accommodate guests.

In the west range, on the end of the kitchen tower, there are several tusks – stones projecting from the tower's face. This suggests that there was another stone structure built against this wall. At the very least this was the intention, and the rough nature of the lower levels of masonry indicates that the tusks were left behind after the adjacent building was dismantled.

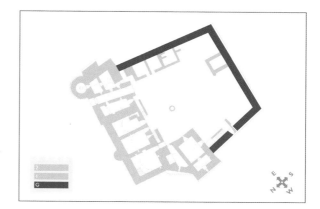

Along the east wall there is no such evidence of high-status chambers: the structures here were less finely built. They may have been used as service accommodation, or included a bakehouse and brewhouse which have not been identified elsewhere on the site. There must also have been a stable for the duke's horses somewhere in the courtyard.

Right: The wall walk at the top of the curtain walls provided a platform from which to defend the castle, and view the surrounding area.

THE KITCHEN TOWER: KITCHEN AND SERVERY

The kitchen and servery are the main rooms we have left which show what life was like for a servant here at Doune. The marks left by knives and tools on the stonework reveal fascinating traces of those who lived and worked here, but who are largely forgotten by historical record.

The oddly-shaped room you first come to at the top of the stairs is the servery. This would have acted as a passage, through which food was passed between the kitchen and servants working in the great hall. To your left are the two serving hatches. They may have had wooden shutters that could be closed when food was not being served. This room was also the principal access for guests to the great hall. It is strange that guests would enter through such a low-status room, and this may be a further indication that Albany was incorporating existing buildings into his work.

Through the door to the right of the serving hatches is the kitchen. One side of the room is dominated by the large, low-arched fireplace, which would have been the focus of activity. The fireplace would have had several fires, all doing different jobs, rather than the single large fire that might be expected. Some of the space would also have been used for storage. The window to the right of the fireplace gave light to those working there. However, it also has a window seat, so it probably also provided a well-lit space in which the pastry chef could craft his intricate designs.

Below: The servery hatches, through which food would be passed on its way between the kitchen and the great hall. They may have had wooden shutters that could be closed when food was not being served.

Below: The large window at the east end of the kitchen. There would most likely have been a shuttered window here, rather than the leaded one we see today.

While the fireplace was the main focus of cooking, some floor space may have been given over to cooking fires as well. Smoke holes above the windows provided ventilation. The present paving dates to the 1880s but paving was not unusual in high-status kitchens. A bread oven, the low footings of which survive by the big east window, was also added after Albany's day, probably during the 1745 Jacobite Rising. The large window is also of a later date – leaded windows were rare in kitchens, as shutters provided better ventilation. The grooves on the wall either side of this window show where kitchen workers sharpened their tools.

Returning to the servery and looking upwards, you can see projecting corbels which supported the upper floors, dividing this section of the tall tower. These rooms are fairly small and lack fireplaces, so they probably accommodated some of the household staff. They were reached from the spiral staircase next to the entrance. This stone stair is a later insertion, though it probably replaces a timber stair in the same place.

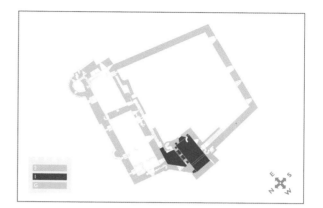

Above: Tool marks on the flank of the kitchen window act as a reminder of those whose life here was to serve, rather than be served.

Above: The large arch of the fire dominates the kitchen.

Above: Men cooking at a fire, from the 1300s manuscript, *The Luttrell Psalter.* The drawing shows how a single fire could be used simultaneously for different purposes.

DID YOU KNOW . . .

Unlike today, pastry was not eaten in the medieval period. It was simply used as a container in which to cook the food and was discarded afterwards.

THE KITCHEN TOWER: UPPER CHAMBERS

Climbing the stairs brings you to one of the best-preserved rooms in the castle. This chamber is traditionally known as 'Mary Queen of Scots' Bedchamber'. Mary may have slept here when she visited on 13 September 1563.

Mary stayed only one night, while travelling from Stirling to Dunblane. Her mother, Mary of Guise, also stayed here in 1545. It is certainly a high-status room, and would have provided suitable accommodation for a member of the royal family. Being above the kitchen, it would have been warm, but it was also furnished with a finely carved fireplace, making it especially cosy.

The room's status is also suggested by the large windows, originally part-glazed above with shutters below. The slight indent on the corner of the fireplace wall may have been intended for holding rush-lights, or tallow candles, with which to illuminate the room. Its usual occupant was probably the chamberlain or steward, who controlled and organised the household – its proximity to the hustle and bustle of the kitchen would have made it unsuitable as long-term accommodation for a royal resident.

Above: The fine detailing on the fireplace in 'Mary Queen of Scots' Bedchamber' makes it likely that this room was used by important guests.

Above: This unusual alcove may have been hollowed out to hold rush-lights, or tallow candles, to illuminate the room.

At one end of the chamber there are two smaller closets. One was a latrine closet. It has been suggested that the other was a sleeping closet, but the space is probably too cramped for this. The doorway, though, is finely carved, suggesting it had some significant purpose. Both rooms would have been warm as they flank the kitchen fireplace flue.

The top floor of this tower is a simple garret, and was accessible only from the wall walk. It would have provided the most basic accommodation. It was sometimes used for housing prisoners, and it may have been from here that John Home and other prisoners escaped in 1746 (see page 44).

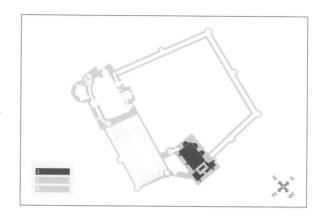

Above: Mary Queen of Scots, who spent a night at Doune in 1563, and dined at the castle the next day. Her visit may have given this room its name.

Left: The latrine chamber off the bedchamber.

THE GREAT HALL

The great hall is the largest room in the castle. Here the majority of the household would have eaten and some minor servants would have slept.

Although the hall is entered through the servery, the doorway is large and finely carved, symbolising entry into a room of high status. Those entering the great hall would first encounter the screens passage. This area is now marked by a low kerb, probably in the same position as the original timber screen, which would have resembled the restored screen in the duke's hall. This separated the service space from the rest of the hall, hiding activities from view and reducing draughts. A door to the left gave access to the minstrels' gallery and to the wall-walks. At the far end of the passage, opposite the door, was a small service room with access to the cellar below.

The hall was restored in the 1880s and much of what you see dates to that period, including the roof, the minstrels' gallery, the glazing and the furniture. The roof beams are supported by corbels carved with a variety of faces. Some of these were restored in the 1880s, and some are the medieval originals. There was evidence of a brazier or firebasket in the centre of the hall – this would have been needed as there are no fireplaces. A similar arrangement exists in the laigh hall of Dundonald Castle in Ayrshire, from the same period. The smoke is vented through a louvred smoke-hole above.

Top: The great hall has a feeling of medieval splendour, yet many of its features date from the restoration of the 1880s. Some of the corbels, the roof and the minstrels' gallery all date from this later period.

Far left: One of the remaining medieval corbels, supporting the roof-beams.

Left: A corbel dating from the 1880s restoration of the castle, probably replacing a similar, medieval one in the same position.

Five windows provide light for the hall, and no two are alike. This suggests that the hall was adapted from existing structures, or that Albany originally had a different plan for this part of the castle. The finest window is at the dais end, where the duke sat, and would have bathed him and his most honoured guests in light. However, it was increasingly rare for a senior nobleman to dine in his main hall in the medieval period: the trend was towards more privacy. He would be represented by a high-ranking household official if he was dining elsewhere. The opening within this window recess was probably a latrine for the exclusive use of the top table. It was most likely a dry closet, as otherwise the contents would have emptied onto guests as they approached the stair. Not a very warm welcome! The stair at the dais end probably led to the wine cellar – only people of high status drank wine with meals.

The hall was probably sparsely furnished, with long tables set up only for meal times and cleared away between servings. Colour and warmth would have been provided by tapestries and hangings on the walls – if you look up you can still see traces of the hooks which supported them.

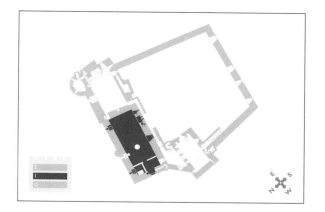

DID YOU KNOW...

Minstrels provided entertainment for those dining in the hall. However, they performed a much more essential service – it was their playing that announced meals were being served in the days before clocks were common.

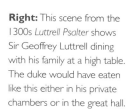

Right: This scene from the 1300s *Luttrell Psalter* shows Sir Geoffrey Luttrell dining with his family at a high table. The duke would have eaten like this either in his private chambers or in the great hall.

THE GATEHOUSE TOWER: THE DUKE'S HALL

The first chamber entered from the great hall is known as the duke's hall.
In the absence of contemporary records it is difficult to know what this
chamber was used for, but educated guesses can be made.

It is thought this was the duke's hall due to the grandness of the architecture and the
room's position adjacent to the great hall. This room provided a more private dining
space, increasingly leaving the great hall to the servants, as well as being a place where
the duke could conduct business. It could be entered directly from the courtyard,
so that the duke and his visitors did not need to pass through the great hall.

The present decor of this chamber dates to the 1880s, giving a misleading impression
of its original appearance. It would have been lavishly decorated, more so than the great
hall, and rich hangings would have adorned the walls. The focal point of the room was
probably a chair of estate, placed near the twin fireplaces and provided with rich hangings,
embellished with the duke's coat of arms and emphasising his status. Here the duke
would also have a cupboard displaying gold and silver plate to show his wealth.

Above: The duke's hall, with its impressive and curious double fireplace, is both magnificently
medieval and eccentrically Victorian. It was extensively restored in the 1880s.

The screens passage at the west end of the hall was installed as part of the restoration, but a similar arrangement probably existed in the medieval castle. It would have concealed the service stair between this chamber and the great hall, also reducing draughts and supporting the minstrels' gallery. The fireplaces are among the surviving glories of this chamber and are very unusual, though it is not clear why this particular design was chosen. The skewed angle of the fireplace wall indicates that Albany was working with existing structures. Also surviving is access to the murder hole you saw in the entrance passage – look under the timber flap in the sill of the north-facing window.

When the duke was dining here a trestle table could be set up for him and his guests. Only the most high-status guests would dine with him – others would be relegated to the great hall.

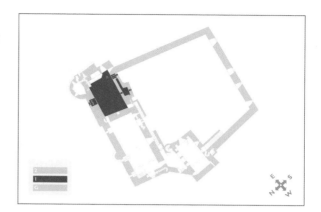

They would, though, have had a chance to see what they were missing, as food for the duke's table would be processed past them. Food was an important way of asserting status – the higher your rank, the greater the quality and variety of food you would be served.

Above: The duke's hall as it might have looked in Albany's day.

THE GATEHOUSE TOWER:
THE DUKE'S HALL (CONTINUED)

Medieval halls often served multiple functions. As well as providing an intimate dining space for the duke and his senior guests, the hall may have been used as an ante-room, or for administering justice.

The duke's hall would also have been a place where important men could wait for the duke when he was in his study. A hatch in the floor to the right of the fireplaces gave access to the cellars, allowing food and drink to be transported here directly, to offer them basic sustenance. The small mural chamber in the south wall provided space for a porter or usher to prepare food for service, and a drain for waste disposal and hand washing. Although the usher could have observed those waiting, it was not primarily a means of spying, as is sometimes thought.

In the north wall, steps lead down to small chamber. The changing floor level here has been taken as further evidence that Albany was adapting existing structures. Within the chamber there are more signs of alteration. The vaulted ceiling is inserted – it cuts the doorway and so was clearly built later. Also, there is a partially blocked arrow-slit, with the wide embrasure, or recess, still evident. From here, a defender could have safely fired upon unwanted visitors.

The hatch in the floor leads to the lowest level of the round tower, the possible pit prison. Symbolic acts had great value in the medieval period and the lowering of a prisoner into the prison after receiving judgement from the duke would have been a powerful representation of lordly justice. More macabre still, outside the castle gates there was once a great ash tree, known as the gallows tree, where wrong-doers were reputedly hanged. It blew down in November 1878, but furniture was made from its wood, some of which remains in the duke's hall.

Right: Some of the remaining furniture in the duke's hall is made from the wood of the gallows tree – a reminder of the different ways justice has been enforced over the years.

DID YOU KNOW...

As well as being military and administrative centres, castles acted as local courts: lords had a duty to exert justice over those living within their lands. In the castle, evidence would be presented and sentence passed. The castle would also provide a space in which to hold those found guilty. Rich and powerful offenders may have been given quite comfortable quarters. The less fortunate would find themselves in pit prisons.

Left: A French medieval noble administering justice to those within his jurisdiction. Nobles kept order, according to the Crown's instructions.

VICTORIAN RESTORATION

The 1800s saw increasing amounts of activity in the restoration of historic buildings. Arguments raged about the methods and principles behind it.

Through the century, unease grew over the manner in which restoration was undertaken, particularly in the case of ecclesiastical monuments. An 1874 report stated that there were very few remaining examples which had not seen some level of restoration. It has been said that more medieval architecture was lost through restoration than through demolition. While some efforts were based on detailed research (and the work here at Doune is among the better examples), there was a growing belief that even these alterations were destructive. In their efforts to return a monument to a fictitious ideal state, the restorers obscured its construction history.

Some societies and individuals spoke out against such work. The art critic, John Ruskin, was a particularly vocal opponent. In 1849 he wrote that restoration meant 'the most total destruction which a building can suffer' and felt that where repairs were necessary they should be done honestly and without pretence. Indeed, 'truth' and 'memory' were two of the 'seven lamps of architecture' he enumerated in his book of the same name. William Morris was also an opponent of overzealous restoration. Under his influence the Society for the Protection of Ancient Buildings was created in 1877. Although Morris had initially profited from the amount of restoration taking place, he was increasingly disturbed by the destruction involved.

This growing concern culminated in the first legislation in Britain aimed at preserving ancient monuments, with the Ancient Monuments Protection Act of 1882. Though the Act was very limited in scope, it marked the first legislative efforts to protect monuments which we now take for granted. Ironically, societies now exist which seek to preserve the endeavours of the Victorian restorers whose work led to the legislation in the first place.

Top: The writer and art critic, John Ruskin, was one of the most vehement speakers in support of protecting ancient buildings from overzealous restorers.

Above: Doune Castle, illustrated by Robert Billings around 1850, before the major restoration of the 1880s. The roofs and well-head that we see today are two of the most obvious Victorian additions.

THE GATEHOUSE TOWER: UPPER CHAMBERS

Top: The fireplace in what may have been the duke's private study.

Above: The piscina in the oratory of the upper hall. This was probably used for worship only by the family and their intimate friends.

Above: The restored fireplace in the great hall of Linlithgow Palace.

As with the duke's hall, evidence showing how the upper chambers of the gatehouse tower were used is scarce. However, we can guess based on what we know of medieval ideas of precedence.

The first chamber you come to, although previously thought to be the duke's bedchamber, was probably his study. Here he could attend to business too private for his hall, or else retire while his hall was prepared for dining. He could of course also eat here if he wanted to. With its part-glazed windows, fine fireplace and en suite garderobe, this is certainly a room designed for the duke's private use.

Continuing up the stairs, you arrive at a similar chamber, though without a fireplace or a private latrine. It probably provided space for those waiting to enter the grand hall beyond. As one of the most lavish spaces in the castle, this hall was probably the duke's bedchamber. To the left as you enter is a large fireplace, which shows evidence of having once been hooded, similar to the restored fireplace in the great hall at Linlithgow Palace. The large windows, with evidence of glazing and iron bars, also suggest the high status of the room.

Opposite the fireplace was space for the bed of estate, from which the duke may have conducted business, as was the fashion in Europe at that time. On the courtyard wall is an alcove that was once screened off from the rest of the hall (you can still see evidence of this on the east side of the alcove).

In the alcove's east wall there is a small oratory, or chapel, containing a triangular headed credence for storing consecrated vessels, and an octagonal piscina for washing them. The size and location suggests this was a private chapel for the duke and his intimates. In records, there is mention of two chapels at Doune, both dedicated to St Fillan. One of these was within the walls, and one outside by the river. It is highly unlikely that the internal one mentioned was the small, private oratory we see today. It has been suggested, therefore, that there may have been a chapel in the south-east corner of the courtyard, lit by the largest window. This lends further weight to the theory that the buildings against the south curtain wall were completed.

Around the walls are the remains of projecting corbels which supported the floor above. The top floor was divided into separate chambers, two of which have large windows and latrines. This suggests they were important rooms despite lacking fireplaces. It is possible that central hearths were used to heat them. They were probably the duchess's chambers.

Continuing up the stair you come to the battlements. There would have been a full height chamber here, which is now lost. You can still appreciate the stunning views across the landscape. This was an important part of medieval castle setting – the ability to see and be seen.

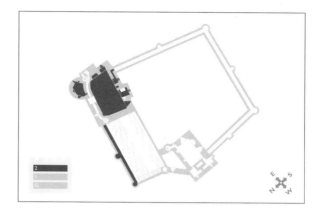

Below: The view from the battlements, looking over the River Teith, retains the dramatic impact that it would have had in Albany's day.

THE CASTLE EXTERIOR

When you have finished exploring the castle's rooms, take a walk
around the walls. This is an excellent way to appreciate its scale and setting.

Around the walls, there are further features which suggest that there was a structure
here, pre-dating Albany. Leaving the gateway and turning right, you come to a round
tower. Looking up, you can see the latrine closet serving the duke's study projecting from
the wall. Just below it and to the right are the remains of a blocked arrow-slit in the form
of a cross. These features are usually of earlier date than most of the buildings at Doune.
Also, on the square tower projecting behind the round tower, there is a clear difference
in the nature of the quoins, or corner stones, at either side. The lower levels of stonework
are different to those above, indicating they belong to a different phase of building.

Left: The west curtain wall of the castle.
Here we can see the blocked postern gate
(bottom right) and latrine closets projecting
from the walls. It is also possible to make out,
where the shadow hits the wall, a change in
stonework. This leads experts to believe that
parts of this wall may belong to an earlier
construction on the site.

The outside of the east curtain wall is as plain as the courtyard side. The only breaks are provided by water spouts, the parapet and round turrets that project from the wall-head. These features were added during James VI's repairs of the 1580s.

Continuing around to the south of the castle, there are excellent views of the River Teith on the right. The banks and ditches sloping away from the castle may have been part of the defences of the castle or an earlier fort. They may also be natural landscape features or remnants of a garden. We just don't know without excavation of this area.

The west curtain wall is very plain, but you can see the outline of the blocked postern gate, a small service door. Above it is a machicolation, or stone box, which allowed guards to fire down on attackers. The three latrine chutes visible further along the wall may also have been used for this purpose if necessary. The middle latrine services the high-status room in the kitchen tower. The lower one is a twin-seater, probably for kitchen staff. The upper latrine was probably also for use by servants – they would have had to go out onto the battlements to access it – their comfort clearly wasn't very important! On the projecting kitchen tower you can see that the lower courses of stonework are different from the upper stories and are probably part of an earlier building.

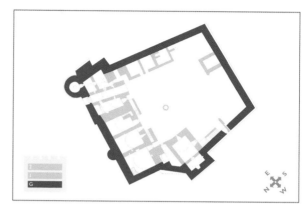

Returning to the north of the castle, you skirt the outside of the great hall. Here there are more unknowns. We don't know the purpose of the projecting round tower – it may have been intended to support a cross wall behind it, which either wasn't built or has been entirely removed. This and the varying levels and styles of the great hall windows suggest at the very least that Albany made changes during construction. Alternatively, alterations have been made to existing chambers to create the large hall that exists today.

While the area outside the castle is now mainly open space, evidence exists that there were previously buildings here. It is likely that in Albany's time many service buildings occupied this space. However, the lack of detailed archaeological investigation makes it difficult to know the location or date of structures in this area. One hint that still remains is a structure thought to be an icehouse to the north-east of the castle entrance.

Left: The ice-house to the north-east of the gatehouse. Although it is a later addition, it serves as a reminder of the ancillary buildings that stood close to the castle in its later period.

THE HISTORY OF DOUNE CASTLE

This page: The south curtain wall, pierced with fine windows.

We do not know whose castle this was originally, but Doune is most closely associated with Robert Stewart, Duke of Albany, and its imposing presence beside the River Teith emphasises his power and wealth.

Albany was a member of the royal house of Stewart. Although he was never king himself, he held the reins of government of Scotland for a total of 22 years between 1388 and 1420, and was a key political figure throughout the period.

The first references to Doune Castle occur in documents dated 1381, and it was presumably habitable by 1401 when Albany wrote letters from here to Henry IV of England. We now also think that there was a castle on this site before Albany's time. He was certainly not the only one to see the advantages of this strategic location and following his death the castle and its surroundings would be enjoyed by many Stewart monarchs.

THE SETTING, THE ROMAN FORT AND THE DUN

Doune Castle is strategically situated on a promontory formed by a meeting of the River Teith and the Ardoch Burn. The importance of the location was clearly recognised from very early times, judging by evidence of earlier activity in the area.

The Romans certainly appreciated the strength of the position, constructing a timber and earth fort on the level ground just to the north of the castle, between the castle and the present village of Doune. The fort probably dates to the period just after the invasion of Agricola in the first century AD. It is rectilinear in shape and is visible in aerial photographs as cropmarks. It was only discovered in 1983, with excavations in 1984, 1999, 2008, 2010 and 2011 revealing that it is excellently preserved. The area is now used by the Doune Cricket Club.

Because the Roman fort is in such good condition, there is reason to hope that future surveys will establish whether there were fortifications on the site before the present castle was built. For the time being, we need to rely on other techniques such as place-name evidence. The name 'Doune' suggests that this was the case: the word derives from 'dun' or 'doon', meaning an ancient stronghold. The ditches and banks that cross the promontory may well belong to an earlier fort. Recent surveys of the surviving stonework add weight to the theory that there was a castle on the site before Albany's time in the 1390s.

Above: A Roman cavalry harness mount found during excavations at the fort in 2010.

Left: An aerial shot of Doune Roman fort – now the village's cricket pitch. You can just make out the outline of the camp in cropmarks.

Above: Doune Castle, sitting between the River Teith and the Ardoch Burn. Its position makes it strong and easily defensible.

TIMELINE

AD 79	c.500–c.600 AD

AGRICOLA'S armies push north into Caledonia, modern-day Scotland, and establish several forts; amongst them Doune.

A LOCAL DUN or tribal fort possibly stood on the site of the present Doune Castle.

THE CASTLE BEFORE THE DUKE OF ALBANY

The focus on Doune as the product of Albany's time has obscured from view its potential use in the earlier medieval period. In particular, the castle may have been a main seat and crucial administrative centre of the earldom of Menteith.

From at least the 10th century, Scotland was divided into territories, some of which formed mormaerdoms, later called earldoms. Mormaers were second only to the king in stewardship and authority. These seats of power included Menteith, which stretched between the Rivers Teith and Forth.

Although the precise geographic composition of the earldom is unclear, there is significant evidence to support the inclusion of lands around Doune as a major portion of its eastern flank. Inchtalla, an island castle in the Lake of Menteith, is usually considered the main seat of the earldom, and it certainly was in the period after 1427.

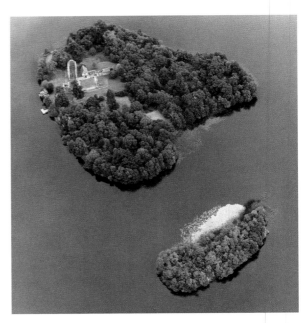

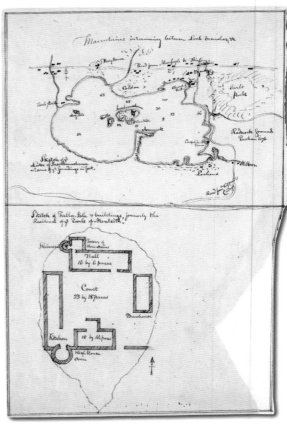

Top right: Inchtalla, once the main seat of the earldom of Menteith, next to the larger island of Inchmahome in the Lake of Menteith.

Above: Doune's south front, seen from the other side of the River Teith.

Right: Sketch-plan of the buildings that were once visible on Inchtalla, by Reverend John Sime c.1840.

In the 1200s the earldom was dominated by two families: the Comyns, centred on Inchtalla, and the Stewarts, whose main seat in the earldom is of unknown location. The Stewarts were the earls of Menteith, and would certainly have had a base within the province. Indeed, we know that the 'main seat of the earldom' was explicitly granted to the Stewarts in 1285, when Inchtalla was most definitely in Comyn hands. This 'main seat' must therefore have been another castle.

It seems very probable that this was Doune. Castles were not just military fortifications but also had an important role as administrative centres. It would have been necessary for the earl to construct a residence to control the resources and gather the revenues of the estate and, for this, Doune would be the most logical location. This strongly supports the idea that there was a castle here prior to Albany's dominance in the later 1300s.

The Teith was a major salmon river in the medieval period and an important source of income. Doune Castle was likely situated here to take advantage of this. The promontory on which the castle sits also provided views of the important hunting forests which formed part of the earldom. Hunting was a favourite noble pastime as well as a means of providing food for the table.

The Stewart earls would also have been well aware of the symbolic benefits of castle-building as a means of cementing their control, as evidenced by their seats in the west of Scotland such as Rothesay and Dundonald.

Above: The laigh hall at Dundonald Castle. Dundonald was once a main seat of the Stewarts on the west coast of Scotland. The hall has air vents that show braziers were used to heat the room, as in the great hall at Doune.

DID YOU KNOW ...

The River Teith is famous for its excellent fishing. In 1919 a recently discharged soldier, Peter Ferguson, caught a 40lb salmon near the castle – four times the average weight.

1124 | **1314**

DAVID I comes to the throne of Scotland. Under his influence, Norman systems of castle-building and feudalism flourish.

ROBERT THE BRUCE Albany's great-grandfather, defeats the English at the Battle of Bannockburn.

THE RISE OF ROBERT STEWART

The man who would become Duke of Albany, and who built the castle we see today, seems to have gained much respect in his lifetime. However, history has cast a rather disapproving eye on his actions. Whatever we can infer about his character, one thing is certain – his position was achieved and maintained with formidable political acumen.

Robert Stewart was born around 1340, a younger son of Robert II and his first wife Elizabeth Mure of Rowallan. Robert II, the founder of the Stewart dynasty, came to the throne in 1371 and faced considerable challenges controlling his kingdom.

A major part of the problem was the large number of children he had. By 1382, eight out of fifteen earldoms in Scotland were controlled by Robert's sons. While placing a loyal noble in a turbulent area could have been advantageous, in reality Robert's sons were more concerned with building their own authority than with supporting their father's. In the vying for power it was Robert's eldest son John, Earl of Carrick who initially triumphed, leading a coup to remove the king from effective power in 1384. Carrick would, however, eventually be forced to give way to his younger brother, our Robert Stewart, who took control after Carrick was injured by a horse-kick in 1388.

Left: The Battle of Otterburn, as illustrated in Froissart's *Chronicles* of the 1470s. The Earl of Douglas, powerful friend and ally of John, Earl of Carrick, was killed in the battle in 1388, weakening Carrick and allowing Albany to gain power.

Robert was perfectly placed to gain power. He was the son of the king, married well, and was politically shrewd. His marriage to Margaret Graham had given him control of the earldom of Menteith in 1361. Then, royal descent, combined with his own adept manoeuvring, helped him gain control of the earldom of Fife in 1372, and the constableship of Stirling Castle the following year. It also gained him the position of chamberlain, the chief financial officer of the kingdom, in 1382.

Later, Robert exploited the weaknesses of both the king and Carrick to become guardian of Scotland. Carrick had lost support following his injury, and the death of his powerful ally James Douglas, 2nd Earl of Douglas and Mar, at the Battle of Otterburn. In 1388 a general council chose Robert 'for putting into effect justice and keeping the law internally, and for the defence of the kingdom' due to 'the great and numerous defects in [its] governing'. Robert Stewart was now essentially running Scotland.

His tenure was to continue until Carrick recovered his health or Carrick's son, David, was of age. The council retained him as guardian even once Carrick became Robert III in 1390. It was only in 1393 when David, the new Earl of Carrick, began to increase his influence that Robert's initial term of guardianship came to an end.

Above: John, Earl of Carrick who became King Robert III in 1390. His physical and political weakness prevented him ever really gaining control of the kingdom.

DID YOU KNOW . . .

When John, Earl of Carrick became king in 1390, he chose the name Robert III. This clearly identified him with the dynasty of his great-grandfather Robert the Bruce. But it also sidestepped a problem. The previous King John had been a member of the rival Balliol family. His right to rule had been widely disputed and he had been forced to abdicate in 1296. If the new king took the title John I, he would be openly denying Balliol's kingship. As John II, he would acknowledge it. The name was therefore better avoided.

1371

ROBERT II
the father of Albany, comes to the throne.

1386

ALBANY
becomes Governor of Scotland.

THE UNCROWNED KING

David, Earl of Carrick, initially with the support of his father Robert III, increased his influence during the 1390s, culminating in his creation as Duke of Rothesay in 1398. However, Robert Stewart continued to be powerful, and he was named Duke of Albany at the same ceremony.

Both titles reflect the great power of the two men. Rothesay Castle was one of the main seats of Stewart power on the west coast, so David's choice of title reflected the family's dominance. It also associated the prince with the front line of defence against the Lords of the Isles, whose frequent attacks on mainland Scotland were an ever-present source of conflict.

Albany's choice of title has been seen as a sign of his kingly ambitions. 'Albany' derives from 'Alba', now used to mean the whole of Scotland. However, then 'Alba' referred to the ancient heart of the kingdom north of the Forth and south of Moray. The title can therefore be seen as a justifiable reference to Stewart's territorial lordship in the region, and his association with Fife and lands in the north. As with Rothesay's, Albany's title must be seen in the context of royal efforts to resist the power of the lordship of the Isles in the west and north.

Above: A map showing the historic region of Alba, from which modern Scotland developed. The Duke of Albany's title was inspired by this ancient heartland. We can only draw approximate boundaries, but we know that it was bordered by the River Spey in the north and the River Forth in the south.

Rothesay was described as 'plesand and mychty' by the contemporary poet and chronicler Andrew Wyntoun. He achieved recognition of his ascendancy in 1399, when he was appointed as the king's lieutenant, his father being unable to 'exert himself to govern the realm'. Yet again Albany held his influence, being appointed to the advisory council to which Rothesay had to report. It was also Albany who became guardian after Rothesay died in 1402, despite being implicated in his demise (see pages 38–9).

In 1406 Albany achieved his most powerful position, being appointed Governor of Scotland. Robert III had died and his heir, James, younger brother of David, was a hostage in England. Scotland was therefore without a resident monarch. As next in line to the throne, and with a proven track record of leadership, Albany was the obvious choice to fill this position. He was a highly effective governor and attracted much praise from contemporaries: the historian Abbot Walter Bower refers to the 'honourable fashion' of his governorship. He certainly fulfilled the requirements of a medieval ruler, personally leading an armed force against the Lord of the Isles in 1412.

Above: Rothesay Castle, from which the Duke of Rothesay took his title. It was one of the main Stewart seats of power on the west coast, and part of the line of defence against the Lords of the Isles.

1390

ROBERT III, Albany's elder brother, succeeds to the throne of Scotland.

1399

DAVID, DUKE OF ROTHESAY challenges Albany's authority over Scotland and is appointed king's lieutenant.

A TARNISHED REPUTATION

Despite his competence as governor and his popularity with many of his contemporaries, Albany's reputation has taken a distinct beating over time. Walter Bower praised his generosity and wisdom, but the duke has been painted as a wicked uncle, concerned only with ensuring his own position at the expense of his brothers and nephews. One of the biggest stains on his reputation is his association with the death in 1402 of his nephew, David, Duke of Rothesay.

David was heir to the throne, and had been acting with increasing force and independence. Having existed without the rule of a strong king for some time, Albany and other members of the Scottish nobility were worried by his aggressive assertion of royal power. With support, Albany engineered his arrest late in 1401. David was imprisoned at St Andrews before being moved to Albany's castle at Falkland. He died there in March 1402.

The exact circumstances of David's death are unclear: Bower writes that 'after languishing with dysentery or (as some would have it) with hunger he died'. Although Albany was not present, there were those who believed him responsible. In May of the same year, a general council declared Albany 'to be innocent, harmless, blameless, quit, free and immune completely in all respects from the charge' and stated that there should be no further 'murmurings' against him. The clear implication is that rumours were already spreading and Albany had to act to suppress them. They were clearly not enough to harm his political standing.

Above: Falkland Palace developed in the 1500s from the earlier Falkland Castle. The castle was one of the Duke of Albany's main residences. His nephew, David, Duke of Rothesay, died there in 1402.

Albany's reputation has also suffered from his failure to secure the release of his other nephew, the future King James I, from English captivity. It has been thought that, wanting to hold onto power, he conspired to keep James captive, or at least did not try to pay the ransom. An indenture he sealed in 1409 contained the phrase 'gif it happynnis the said lorde, Duc Albany, to grow in tyme to the estate of king', is often used as evidence of his ambition. However, he was the nearest male relative to a captive, uncrowned king with no children, so he was quite likely to come to the throne naturally.

Albany's failure to obtain James's release is perhaps understandable. It is true that he managed to gain the freedom of his own son, Murdoch, but Henry IV and Henry V of England would have been much less willing to give up a hostage as valuable as the king of Scots. It was only with the uncertain political situation in England after the death of Henry V that they were willing to negotiate a ransom for James.

'He was the most patient of all men, gentle enough and kind, talkative and friendly, a daily attender at feasts, outstanding beside all his companions, a man who was a big spender and generous to strangers. He was also distinguished in appearance, tall and lofty in body, gray-haired in appearance and understanding, lovable in countenance, gifted with prudence and bravery, famous for his discretion, unremitting in his forbearance'

Abbot Walter Bower of Inchcolm, quoted in his
Obituary of Robert Stewart, Duke of Albany,
published around 1440.

Far left: James I of Scotland, younger brother of David, Duke of Rothesay, was held in captivity in England for 18 years before assuming power in Scotland.

Left: Henry V of England. His death threw the country and monarchy into turmoil, and made it possible for James I to gain freedom and return to Scotland.

1402

1420

ROBERT III's son David, Duke of Rothesay dies in Albany's care at Falkland Castle.

ALBANY DIES on 3 September in Stirling Castle, and is buried at Dunfermline Abbey.

AFTER ALBANY

When Albany died in 1420, his titles, his lands and the governorship of Scotland passed to his son, Murdoch. Unfortunately, Murdoch was less politically adept than his father and the changing situation in Scotland and in England culminated in James I's return to Scotland in 1424. His return was not wholly welcomed by the Scottish nobility, who had little option but to accept the situation.

An objective study may absolve Robert and Murdoch of conspiring to keep James a captive, but the king was clearly suspicious of his cousin. Following his return, he acted to destroy the power of the new duke and his family. The end result was the execution of Murdoch, his son and his father-in-law in May 1425. Doune Castle became a possession of the Crown.

The castle now became a royal retreat. It made an attractive hunting-lodge, convenient for Stirling Castle, and close to the hunting forests of Glenfinlas, near Callander, and the Braes of Menteith, near Aberfoyle. Its location no doubt also explains the castle's inclusion in the marriage portion of successive queens. James II's queen, Mary of Guelders, was granted it in 1449, James III's queen, Margaret of Denmark, in 1468 (in part-exchange for the remaining Norwegian lands in Orkney and Shetland that she brought to the marriage), and James IV's queen, Margaret Tudor, in 1503.

A series of royal keepers were appointed to maintain the castle, using income from its lands to carry out repairs. There are only a few entries in the royal accounts for works, including repairs to the stables in 1434 and a brewery built in 1467. However, these were essential components of a royal residence, and consideration of them indicates that Doune still held some importance. Nevertheless, the work was clearly not enough, and by the end of the 1500s Doune was badly in need of attention.

Top right: Mary of Guelders, wife of James II, the first queen to be given Doune Castle as part of her marriage portion in 1449.

Right: James VI, who breathed new life into the castle in 1580 by commissioning a series of repairs, some of which can still be seen today.

Far left: Margaret of Denmark, who received Doune in her marriage settlement in 1468, in part-exchange for Orkney and Shetland, which she brought to her marriage with James III.

Left: Margaret Tudor, James IV's queen, who was given control of Doune in her marriage agreement of 1503.

It was a young James VI who breathed new life into the castle. In 1580 he noted that 'at our last repairing [retiring] towart our castell and place of Doune in Menteith, we persavit [perceived] the samin and fields thereabout to be maist pleasant for our pastyme and verray commodious for our dwelling in the symmer season'. He also noted the rundown state of the walls and roofs and instructed the keeper to spend the considerable sum of £200 on the repair; in the event, the works cost considerably more. The craftsmanship of Michael Ewing, the stonemason, is still there to be enjoyed, in the corbelled-out parapet on the curtain walls and the attractive round turrets.

1424

JAMES I is ransomed in England and returns to Scotland to take up power.

1425

MURDOCH, 2ND DUKE OF ALBANY, is executed with his son and father-in-law – Doune becomes crown property.

A ROYAL RETREAT

From 1434, a succession of royally appointed keepers were granted income from various lands, fishings and mills associated with the castle, in order to pay for its upkeep and provisions.

William of Moray is the first recorded keeper, though the post passed to the Edmonston family in 1468. In 1520, Margaret Tudor received an obligation, a sealed document, from William Edmonston of Duntreath for the keeping of Doune Castle, and a promise that he would not put a powerful individual or family in charge of the castle. This indicates that the keeper had the authority to appoint others for the day-to-day running of the castle.

However, Duntreath was removed from office after only a few years. In 1525, Margaret wrote to him instructing the castle to be prepared for her arrival. While he agreed to receive the queen, he refused to house her servants. This clearly angered Margaret, and she sought to eject him from his position. He proved reluctant to give it up, despite a decree from the Lords of Council in 1527 and a letter from James V in the same year. The dispute only came to an end in 1532 after a complex round of litigation, by which time Margaret's new brother-in-law James Stewart had been appointed keeper. He retained the position until his death in 1544: he was killed in Dunblane during a brawl with Duntreath and his supporters.

James was succeeded by his son, also James, who had a somewhat colourful career. Implicated in the murder of David Riccio, Mary Queen of Scots' favourite, he was later accused of supporting her following her abdication in 1567. In 1570, he was ordered to surrender Doune Castle. He refused, leading to the first siege in its history by a force under Regent Lennox. After three days James Stewart surrendered the castle on the condition that it would not be destroyed. He was later re-instated, and was created Lord Doune in November 1581, in recognition of his role. His son inherited the title of Earl of Moray through his wife Elizabeth, and became known as the Bonny Earl. Doune Castle remains in the hands of the earls of Moray and lords of Doune to this day.

Above: A ring found during excavations at Doune, dating from the late 1500s or early 1600s.

Above: Margaret Tudor, wife of James IV, was involved in a difficult round of litigation to eject Edmonston of Duntreath from his post as keeper of Doune.

THE BONNY EARL

'O lang will his lady
Look oer the castle Down
Eer she see the Earl of Murray
Come sounding thro the town!'

This verse from the popular folk ballad, 'The Bonny Earl of Murray', listed as Child Ballad 181 in Francis J. Child's *The English and Scottish Popular Ballads*, recounts one of the grislier events in Doune's history.

The bonny earl of the title was James Stewart, 2nd Lord Doune and 2nd Earl of Moray. Moray was famously handsome, and was described by the unknown author of *The Historie and Life of King James the Sext* as 'a cumlie personage, of a great stature and strang of bodie'. After a campaign in the north and a subsequent feud with George Gordon, 1st Marquis of Huntly, he was caught in a siege at his mother's castle in Donibristle on 7 February 1592. Though accounts vary, it seems that the castle was set alight by Huntly's men and, though Moray escaped the flames, he was pursued and killed among rocks by the sea. Folklore has it that, as he lay dying, the earl looked up at Huntly and said, 'Ye've spoiled a better face than your own.'

Moray's mother took his corpse to Leith, where he lay unburied for many months as his supporters pursued justice for his murder. His mother also commissioned a painting of his dead body, showing the wounds he received, beneath the words 'God Revenge My Caus'. Huntly never stood trial.

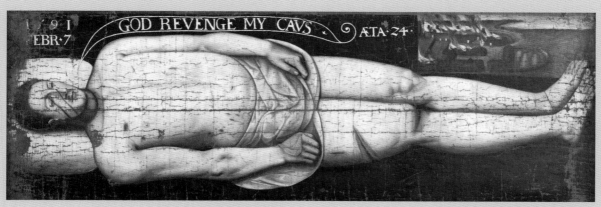

1591
EBR·7   GOD REVENGE MY CAVS   ÆTA·24·

1434

MARY OF GUELDERS future queen of Scotland and custodian of Doune is born, in the same year that the castle's first Royal Keeper, William Moray, is appointed.

1567

JAMES STEWART, refuses to relinquish the castle as it undergoes the first siege in its history.

ESCAPE FROM DOUNE CASTLE

During the wars in the 1560s and 70s, following the abdication of Mary Queen of Scots, Doune had been garrisoned by the Regent Lennox for the imprisonment of the queen's supporters. In the 1700s and 1800s, the castle's strength once more led to its use as a state prison, during which time some prisoners mounted a hazardous escape.

The castle was occupied by government troops during the 1689 and 1715 Jacobite Risings. However, it was the Jacobites who garrisoned Doune during the 1745 Rising. It was held for Prince Charles Edward Stuart (Bonnie Prince Charlie) by MacGregor of Glengyle. Glengyle was in charge of government prisoners lodged at the castle, including several captured following the Jacobite victory at Falkirk early in 1746.

These prisoners included two rather remarkable men: John Home and John Witherspoon. They were held in the rooms above the kitchen, and their daring escape is told by Home in his

History of the Rebellion of 1745. He narrates how he and others knotted sheets to form a rope and climbed from the battlements. The rope broke, but one, Thomas Barrow, was so reluctant to be left behind that he climbed down anyway and fell over 20 feet, dislocating his ankle and breaking several ribs.

Another, Neil Macvicar, the last to descend, attempted to fix the rope by adding extra blankets. Unfortunately he added too many and the rope became too thick to hold. As a result he fell and was 'so grievously hurt, bruised and maimed' that he never recovered, dying of his injuries.

Right: A shoe buckle, probably dating from the late 1600s or 1700s, found in the recent excavations at Doune.

JOHN HOME
(1722–1808)
Born in Leith, Home studied at Edinburgh and in September 1745 enlisted with a group of volunteers to protect the city from Jacobite attack. Thereafter he joined Sir John Cope's army at Dunbar, leading to his capture at Falkirk. Following his escape from Doune Castle he became a minister and a somewhat erratic playwright, his works dividing critical opinion. In 1757 he moved to London where he became private secretary to the Earl of Bute and tutor to the Prince of Wales.

JOHN WITHERSPOON
(1723–94)
Witherspoon studied theology before becoming a Church of Scotland minister. From 1745 he preached in Beith where he joined a group of anti-Jacobite volunteers. He was captured at Falkirk, having gone 'from curiosity to see a battle'. This led to his imprisonment at Doune. In 1768 he accepted the presidency of the Presbyterian College of New Jersey, later known as Princeton University. He was the college's sixth president and a signatory of the Declaration of Independence. John Adams called him 'as high a son of liberty as any man in America'.

THE 14TH EARL OF MORAY

Following its use during the '45, Doune Castle became increasingly ruinous, though it gained popularity as a tourist attraction for visitors going to the Trossachs. A local newspaper reported in 1859 that 'scarcely a day passes without large parties of travellers surrounding it … and every nook and corner of the building is pregnant with strange historical reminiscences.' The picturesque ruin clearly had a strong appeal.

To conserve the building and make it safe for visitors, the 14th Earl of Moray appointed the architect Andrew Kerr to begin restoration work in 1883. Kerr had worked at HM Office of Works, specialising in ancient monuments. He was instructed to keep his work sympathetic to the medieval fabric and was largely successful, at least within the context of the Victorian understanding of medieval buildings.

The restoration generated a great deal of interest, the Glasgow Archaeological Society visiting to view the work in 1883 and again in 1888. They commented on 'the care and taste' with which the work was executed.

Left: George Philip Stuart, 14th Earl of Moray.

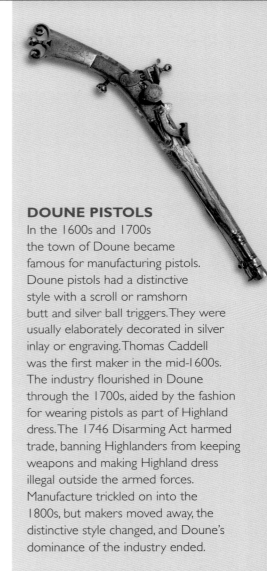

DOUNE PISTOLS

In the 1600s and 1700s the town of Doune became famous for manufacturing pistols. Doune pistols had a distinctive style with a scroll or ramshorn butt and silver ball triggers. They were usually elaborately decorated in silver inlay or engraving. Thomas Caddell was the first maker in the mid-1600s. The industry flourished in Doune through the 1700s, aided by the fashion for wearing pistols as part of Highland dress. The 1746 Disarming Act harmed trade, banning Highlanders from keeping weapons and making Highland dress illegal outside the armed forces. Manufacture trickled on into the 1800s, but makers moved away, the distinctive style changed, and Doune's dominance of the industry ended.

1745

1883

PRINCE CHARLES EDWARD STUART
appoints MacGregor of Glengyle governor of Doune during the last Jacobite Rising.

THE 14TH EARL OF MORAY
appoints Andrew Kerr as architect to survey and restore Doune.

MONTY PYTHON AT DOUNE

'Doune Castle's severe granite halls are now filled with about twenty girls in diaphanous white gowns, shivering against the cold … The bathing scene takes about two hours to set up – the girls giggle a lot, and generally it's about as sexy as a British Legion parade.'

Michael Palin, *Diaries 1969–1979: The Python Years*

Left: Michael Palin on the set of *Monty Python and the Holy Grail*.

In recent years, Doune has continued to attract tourists. In 1975 the castle provided a location for the film *Monty Python and the Holy Grail*, and it has since become a place of pilgrimage for Monty Python fans. Because of tight budgets, Doune was the setting for several different locations: Swamp Castle, Castle Anthrax and Camelot scenes were all filmed here.

The gatehouse pend provided a suitable hiding place for the winch that pulled the Trojan rabbit up the slope to the main entrance, while the courtyard provided the setting for Herbert's wedding day festivities. The large kitchen fireplace was decorated to become the bedroom in which Sir Galahad was examined by two lady doctors. The kitchen was also the room which Sir Galahad accidentally stumbled into during bath-time and from which he was rescued, against his better judgement, by Sir Lancelot.

The great hall provided the backdrop for one of the funniest song and dance routines in film history in the 'Knights of the Round Table' scene. The cast and crew had only one day to film the entire number, which required around 40 different shots. You can hear some of these scenes on the audio tour, narrated by Terry Jones, the film's co-director and co-star. Many of the extras were visitors to Doune who were persuaded to dress up. Costume is strictly optional for visitors today!

In 1984, Doune Castle came in to the care of the State from the Moray Estate under a 999-year lease. Since then, it has continued to attract both visitors and filmmakers. The BBC filmed scenes for the 1997 adaptation of Walter Scott's *Ivanhoe* here, and in 2009 the US network HBO used the castle to film the pilot for the epic *Game of Thrones*. We can only hope that the castle will continue to provide such entertainment and fascination for the public in years to come.

This page: During the filming of *Monty Python and the Holy Grail*, Swamp Castle, Castle Anthrax and Camelot scenes were all filmed at Doune.

1975

MONTY PYTHON
brings Doune to the big screen when they film *Monty Python and the Holy Grail* here.

1984

DOUNE CASTLE
is leased to the nation on a 999-year lease.

There are a number of Historic Scotland properties close to Doune, a selection of which are shown below.

DUNBLANE CATHEDRAL

Built on an ancient Christian site, the medieval cathedral retains its Gothic exterior and red sandstone tower despite restoration.

↗ In Dunblane just off the B8033

🕐 Open all year

📞 01786 823388

🚗 Approx **5 miles** from Doune Castle

🅿️🚻🕐🎁♿🚫

INCHMAHOME PRIORY AND ISLAND

An idyllic setting in the Lake of Menteith, site of a medieval priory briefly visited by Mary Queen of Scots.

↗ By boat from Port of Menteith 8 miles S of Callander off the A81

🕐 Open April-Oct, with last outward sailing at 3:30pm

📞 01877 385294

🚗 Approx **10 miles** from Doune Castle

🅿️🚻🎁🕐

CASTLE CAMPBELL AND GARDENS

The elegant Lowland seat of the Campbells stands in a commanding position at the top of spectacular Dollar Glen.

↗ At the head of Dollar Glen, 10 miles E of Stirling on the A91

🕐 Open all year. Winter: closed Thursday and Friday

📞 01259 742408

🚗 Approx **20 miles** from Doune Castle

🅿️🚻♿🎁🕐

LINLITHGOW PALACE

The birthplace of Mary Queen of Scots, this stunning pleasure palace between Stirling and Edinburgh was enjoyed by many Stewart monarchs.

↗ In Linlithgow just off the M9

🕐 Open all year

📞 01506 842896

🚗 Approx **25 miles** from Doune Castle

🅿️🚻♿🎁

For more information on all Historic Scotland properties, visit **www.historicenvironment.scot**

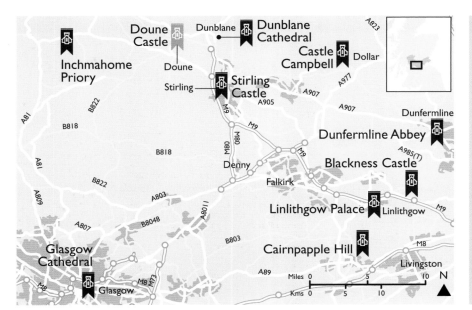

Key to facilities	
Car Parking	🅿️
Accessible by public transport	🚌
Reasonable wheelchair access	♿
Toilets	🚻
Accessible toilets	♿
Interpretive display	📋
Tea/coffee making facilities	☕
May close for lunch	🕐
Shop	🎁
Picnic area	🧺
Strong footware recommended	👢
No dogs	🚫